Manna for Life's Journey

Manna for Life's Journey

*A Selection of Poems and
Song Lyrics to Strengthen the Soul*

I love you Bunky! ~Psalm 1~

Erin Randall Key

Copyright © 2010 by Erin Randall Key.

ISBN:	Softcover	978-1-4535-7330-3
	Ebook	978-1-4535-7331-0

All rights reserved. No part of this book may be reproduced or transmitted in any form or by any means, electronic or mechanical, including photocopying, recording, or by any information storage and retrieval system, without permission in writing from the copyright owner.

This book was printed in the United States of America.

All scripture references are taken from the Authorized King James Version.

To order additional copies of this book, contact:
Xlibris Corporation
1-888-795-4274
www.Xlibris.com
Orders@Xlibris.com

Contents

Preface 9

Subjects:

Life 11

Death/Eternity 29

Christian Service 43

Devotion 55

God's care 71

Waiting 87

Praise 91

Sorrow 97

Jesus 105

Love 117

Trust 133

Repentance 157

Peace 167

Endurance 173

Prayer 189

Many close friends and family members encouraged me to publish a book of my poems and songs, especially my ninety-two year old grandmother, "Meme".
I dedicate this book first of all to her.
Next, I dedicate this work to my parents, Larry and Margaret Randall, who challenge me to use my gifts for God's glory and also to my husband, Jonathan, who never stops believing in me. May this book bring honor to my Lord and Savior, Jesus Christ, who is my true source of joy, strength, and life.

Preface

Words have power to strengthen the soul or to destroy it. Just as healthy food nourishes the body, words of life nourish the soul. God's Word is life, offering daily manna for those who believe. Many of these poems and songs have come as a result of feeding on God's Word and drawing strength from it.

This book's content covers a span of several years, from my childhood to the present. When I was about eight years old, my Mother gave me a beautiful, blank journal, encouraging me to fill it with my thoughts, poems, or drawings. Her gift sparked my imagination and I have been writing ever since. My dream has been to publish what I write in order to encourage others. God is allowing this dream to come true. The purpose of this book is to offer hope and strength for life's journey. My prayer is that God will use each humble selection to bless the heart of the reader.

Some of the selections for this book were inspired by the lives of other Christians. My poem, "Let's Roll" was inspired by 9/11 hero, Todd Beamer. "Lives that Make a Difference" was inspired by my selfless grandmother, "Meme", while "The Greatness of a Man" is a song written in memory of my beloved grandfather, "Pawpaw". "Together" was written for Jonathan while we were preparing for marriage. "A Baby's Beautiful Life" was first written for some friends of mine whose baby boy died at birth. "Hold on" was inspired by the life of missionary James O. Fraser. "The Greatness of a Man" is a song written in memory of my beloved grandfather, "Pawpaw".

At times God has used words spoken in sermons or by a loved one, a phrase read in a book, or simply His creation to inspire ideas for my songs and poems. "The Runner" is a song that my Daddy and I made up when I was a very little girl. We sang it together to the tune of "Chariots of Fire". Life experiences such as getting lost on the Great Wall of China, teaching English classes in Outer Mongolia, feelings of loneliness, loss and longing have also provided inspiration for the selections in this book. There are no wasted experiences. Every circumstance in our lives can be used for good and God's glory if offered to Him. This little book is a simple offering. If only one life is touched, challenged, or encouraged to live for Christ, then this book will have served it's purpose.

Life

Living Today

Dreams about tomorrow
Steal time from today.
Thoughts of future sorrow
Burden and dismay.

There's only enough light
To take the next step.
I live by faith, not sight;
God knows what's ahead.

Trying to figure out
What all lies ahead
Will only wear me out.
I'll trust God instead.

God knows what's best for me.
My life's in His hands.
The future He can see;
Each event is planned.

The more I know God's heart,
The more I'll know peace.
He never will depart
But stays close by me.

Dreams about tomorrow
Aren't reality.
Today I must follow
Christ who died for me.

With one step at a time,
I follow His lead,
Looking to Him I find
Everything I need.

God pours out daily grace
If I'll but receive.
He gives strength for today
In my time of need.

The Manna of God's Word
Is fresh for today.
Daily use of His Sword,
Will Hell's dragons slay.

Christ is the Truth, the Way,
The Abundant Life.
He brings Eternal Day
Dispelling the night.

I choose to live today
Looking unto Him,
And not let my thoughts stray,
But focus on Him!

A Life Challenge

Based on 1 Corinthians 15:58

Every morning when I rise,
I face a brand new day.
To redeem this time is wise,
For it will quickly pass away.

Each trial that life brings,
The labor and the pain,
Gives me reason to sing,
For it is not in vain.

Refrain:
*Therefore, my Beloved Brethren,
Be ye steadfast, unmovable,
Always abounding
In the work of the Lord.
Forasmuch as ye know that your labor
Is not in vain in the Lord.
Forasmuch as ye know that your labor
Is not in vain in the Lord.*

When my time on earth is done,
All tears and sorrow gone,
I will worship Christ the Son
And hear Him say, "Well done."

The Greatness of a Man

My Pawpaw was a man of true greatness.
His life was not marked by fame or success.
My Pawpaw was a man who was selfless,
Serving humanity with gentleness.

Refrain:
The greatness of a man
Can't be measured by size,
Or by power or wealth,
But by what is inside.
A man who is gentle,
Who truly loves the Lord,
Is a man of greatness,
And worthy of reward.

My Pawpaw was a man who loved Jesus.
That legacy of love he passed to us.
My Pawpaw's joy through life was continuous,
Throughout hard times, he was victorious.

My Pawpaw is now at home in Heaven.
We rest in hope that we'll see him again.
We will serve our Lord with love until then.
Like Pawpaw, we will live our lives for Him!

A Life Legacy

As I journey through life
I leave footprints behind
For those who will come after me.

Am I living my life
In a way that will shine,
Investing in eternity?

Each thing I say and do,
All my heart's attitudes
Are forming my life's legacy.

Refrain:
A legacy of faithfulness
A legacy of light
A legacy of love
And a legacy of right
A legacy of Jesus
Living through my life
That's the legacy I want to leave behind.

As I follow my Christ,
Leaving all else behind,
This narrow road won't be easy.

Through the tears I can smile
Knowing it is worthwhile
To live for One who so loves me!

In His presence I find
Joy that boggles the mind.
From trials come testimonies.

I've been given this life
The Lord to glorify.
May I use this brief time wisely.

Lives That Make a Difference

Lives that make a difference
Aren't always plain to see,
Yet their unseen presence
Is felt behind the scenes.

Doing mundane duties,
With joy and thankfulness,
Giving up their own ease,
Willing to be thought less.

With eyes of compassion,
They look for needs to meet.
Loving every person,
They stoop to wash their feet.

It may just be a smile
While passing down life's road,
Or listening a while,
So someone can unload.

A simple word of praise,
A tasty, home-cooked meal,
A heartfelt prayer that's raised
For someone who is ill.

In small and countless ways,
The love of Christ shines through,
Brightening people's days,
By the little things they do.

Lives that make a difference
Aren't the first ones you see.
They're the humble servants
Who sacrifice freely.

Written with His Blood

God has a book with all the names
Of the whole human race.
He keeps account of all we've done.
No word can be erased.

Each secret sin and shortcoming,
Nothing there is hidden.
Words seem to scream out from the page,
This person is condemned!

But when we all were without hope
God sent His only Son
To pay our sin debt with His blood
So our guilt could be gone.

Once by grace, His blood was applied,
It wiped my page all clean.
I'm not an outcast anymore,
I'm a child of the King!

Through adoption I'm known of God,
My name is on His hand.
No more a stranger bound for Hell,
But for the Promised Land!

When the Accuser approaches,
To claim I'm still condemned,
God opens the Lamb's book of Life
And shows my name to Him.

The other book is forgotten,
In the blood of the Lamb,
There is now no condemnation,
I'm saved and *know* I am!

Refrain:
My name is written with His blood,
By Christ's scarred hand upon a page,
Into the Lamb's great Book of Life,
Assuring that I'm truly saved.

Like an Eagle
Based on Romans 6

Above my pain,
Above my pride,
Above my problems,
I will rise with Christ.
By His Spirit and might,
With new life, I'll rise.

Above my self,
Above my sin,
Above temptations,
I will soar with Him.
By feasting on God's Living Word,
He'll help me soar above the world.
To heights unknown and freedom true,
Like an eagle, I'll rise with life anew.

I am alive in Jesus Christ.
I am his servant of righteousness.
For He has bought me with His blood
And captured me by His great love.
I am His child forevermore.
And like an eagle, with Him, I will soar.

Little Things

It's the little things in life
That make it worth the while
Double rainbows in the sky,
A baby's happy smile.

Soft, and gooey mud banks
To sink my toes into,
Helping a freckled faced boy,
Learn how to tie his shoe.

A tall glass of iced peach tea
On a warm afternoon,
Watching baseball and fireworks
And bright hot air balloons.

Homemade vanilla ice cream,
Clean, freshly laundered socks,
A lovely fragrant rose bush,
Waves crashing on the rocks.

Sweet early morning bird songs,
Puffy clouds in the sky,
Riding in the car to church,
Watching the world go by.

A quiet steady rainfall
That refreshes the dry earth,
Shiny copper pennies,
Shared giggles, laughter, mirth.

Snuggling down with a good book,
Wrapped up in a blanket,
Taking a hot bubble bath,
A mug of hot chocolate.

A letter from a dear friend,
Bringing glad sunshine my way,
Looking at picture albums
Remembering past days.

If I will open my eyes,
Blessings richly abound.
Every day in little things,
Such joy is to be found.

Together

Two are better than one
And a three-fold cord
Is not quickly broken.

Our friendship has grown strong
For it's centered on,
It's centered on Jesus.

And I thank Him for the gift of you!
It's all so wonderful and new.
Together we will run life's race
With our eyes fixed upon Christ's face.
Together we will run, together we will run!

Sometimes storm clouds will come
But behind each cloud,
Is bright, shining sun.

Though we can't understand
God's amazing plan,
In His plan we will trust.

We will offer our lives
To serve the Lord
As husband and wife.

May our home be a light
Drawing men to Christ
As we live for Jesus.

Lord, we now commit our lives to you
To honor you in all we do.
Together we will run life's race
With our eyes fixed upon your face.
Together we will run, together we will run!

Death/Eternity

Right This Very Minute

Right this very minute
There are people dying,
Fearing what comes after
They take their final breath.

Right this very minute
There are people crying.
Who will go and tell them
That they need not fear death?

Refrain:
There's no power
In the grave,
For the blood
Of Jesus saves!

There is hope
There is peace
In His love,
All fear's relieved!

Right this very minute
Our lives are a witness
Of Christ who is in us—
The Way, the Truth, the Life.

Right this very minute
The fight for souls wages.
Bearing our cross gladly,
Let us enter the fight!

A Corn of Wheat

Based on John 12:24 and 2 Corinthians 5:17

A corn of wheat lies buried
Beneath the cold, dark earth.
Though outwardly it's hidden
From the ground, there's new birth.

Each corn of wheat is useless,
Without passing through death.
Without a time of burial,
There could be no harvest.

Take time to look around you,
And see the fields white.
Don't forget the harvest comes
From corn of wheat that die.

Each of us must make a choice.
Will we give up our lives,
Choose to suffer with Christ now,
To gain the glorious prize?

The prize of God's high calling,
Through our Lord Jesus Christ,
Who, like a corn of wheat, died,
Giving the world new life,

    Is a most holy calling,
    Which we must labor for.
    God's call involves sacrifice
    Before fruit can be born.

Let's labor for the harvest,
Bearing God's precious Seed,
Daily dying to ourselves,
Seeking souls to reap.

When all the harvest's gathered,
We'll be amazed to find
All the great fruit that has come
From corn of wheat that died.

A Baby's Beautiful Life

The beauty of a baby's life,
Begins before his birth.
From the moment of conception,
His life has matchless worth.

From deep within his mother's womb,
This child can move around,
Stretching his legs, sucking his thumb,
In ways that can astound.

This unborn child can feel and know
His mother's love and care.
Over time, he can recognize
His father's voice, in prayer.

The bond between parent and child
Grows stronger every day.
While awaiting his arrival,
They often pause to pray.

How delicate and how precious,
This tiny little one,
Curled up inside his mother's womb
Their long awaited son.

Yet sometimes, for unknown reasons
God calls a baby home.
His brief life on earth is ended
And his life work is done.

Now safe in Heaven with Jesus
Held in Christ's loving arms,
He is sheltered from all danger,
Free from the world's alarms.

The strong grief his family feels
As they all say goodbye
Reveals the impact his life made
Briefly before he died.

One day they will see him again
But right now, there is pain.
Yet through the tears, they smile and say
Lord, blessed be your name!

Gone Home

Though I have gone, don't grieve for me
For death is not the end!
I've just gone home, with Christ to be,
Your broken heart He'll mend.

I know you're sad that we're apart,
But it will not be long,
Until saints with believing hearts
Will join the heavenly throng.

I will wait at the gate for you.
A twinkling of an eye,
Then you will be coming home too.
See, there's no need to cry.

Bring many others with you here,
Snatching their souls from hell.
Christ's perfect love will cast out fear,
As His good news you tell.

Don't wish me back on earth below.
Heaven is perfect bliss.
Surrounded by loved ones we know,
No place compares to this.

Just hold on fast until Christ comes.
Let no one take your crown.
In His great power and strength you run—
He'll never let you down.

Now wipe away your falling tears.
Replace them with a smile,
For soon you will join me up here.
Life trials will prove worthwhile.

That Great Day

No more crying,
No more goodbyes,
No more dying,
In paradise.

We'll be united
With those we love,
Shouting Hosannas
To Christ above.

All of life's trials
Will fade away
In the bright glory
Of that great day.

Until that day
Let's live with hope
That someday soon
We're going home!

Heaven

Sometimes I feel that I cannot go on.
Fear and doubt plague me and rob me of song.
Darkness around me obscures light of dawn,
Then I remember that for which I long . . .

Heaven, Heaven
Where everything will be renewed,
Heaven, Heaven,
With mansions for me and for you!

My heart is lifted as I think of home,
Where I'll have more joy than I've ever known,
Seeing the fruit of the seeds I have sown,
Casting my crown before Christ on His throne.

Heaven, Heaven
Where all desires are satisfied.
Heaven, Heaven
Where at last my faith will be sight!

Thinking of Heaven helps me to go on,
As I look forward to a brand new dawn.
Forever with Jesus, I'll sing love's song.
Sin, sorrow and sickness will all be gone.

Heaven, Heaven
Where God wipes away every tear.
Heaven, Heaven
No fighting and nothing to fear.

What a grand reunion Heaven will be
When friends and loved ones again we will see.
From death's cruel power we will be set free,
United in love, for eternity.

Heaven, Heaven
Where all of God's people will dwell.
Heaven, Heaven
Where we'll have such stories to tell!

There are untold millions dying today,
Those who are lost will have Hell's price to pay.
Who will give their lives to show them the way?
Who will take the time to witness and pray?

Heaven, Heaven
Where God longs for all men to be.
Heaven, Heaven
Where lame will walk and blind will see.

Nothing that I do for Christ in this life
Will be forgotten in Heaven so bright.
May I be faithful to fight the good fight,
Knowing that one day all will be made right.

    Heaven, Heaven
Where we'll enter into God's rest,
    Heaven, Heaven
Where we will know life at its best.

Such wonders await me on Heaven's shore,
Great riches and beauty unseen before.
Blessings will freely flow from Heaven's store,
But Christ is the central One I will adore.

    Heaven, Heaven
Where we will see Christ face to face.
    Heaven, Heaven
There's not a more wonderful place!

Christian Service

He Can Use Me

Sometimes I think
I'm just too small
To change my world.
I claim to lack
The talents and
The skills to serve the Lord.
I fail to remember
God works great things through the weak.
A tender, broken, contrite heart
Is the only thing He seeks.

Refrain:
If God can use a stone
To cause a giant to fall,
If He can use a shout
To shatter a great wall,
If He can use a rod
To part the vast, Red Sea,
If He can use all these,
Then I know He can use me.

God has given us
Each something
That we can use for Him.
Will we use it for
His purpose or
Will we bury it within?
I want my Heavenly Father
To be pleased and say "Well done."
When He sees I've given all I am
To bring honor to His Son.

Brushstrokes

Across the canvas of eternity
There are many brushstrokes used.
Some of them are small and delicate,
While others are bold and huge.

Each brushstroke's role is important
In the picture that unfolds.
They're swept on by the paint brushes
That are soft, not stiff and old.

The Great Artist of the Universe
Takes these brushes in His hand,
And so skillfully He uses them
To produce His Master plan.

What kind of brush am I?
Am I soft and useable?
Or do I let the cares of life
Make me hard and miserable?

Do I mind if all I'm used for
Is for tiny strokes unseen,
Which enhance His bigger picture
And help to complete the scene?

When my life on earth is finished,
From Heaven's eyes, I will see,
How each brushstroke made a difference
And helped to paint a Masterpiece.

Let's Roll!

Let's Roll!
Let's Roll!
On God's promises
We'll hold.
We'll build our faith
Upon the Rock.
Faith that withstands
All pain and shock.
We'll put our trust
In the One
Who gave us
His precious Son.
He's the One
Who is in control—Let's Roll!

Let's Roll!
Let's Roll!
Let's not look back,
Not lose hope.
With no regrets
Let's live our lives.
With no reserves
Let's sacrifice.
With no retreats
Pay the price,
Filled with hope
That never dies,
The hope of
Life in Jesus Christ—Let's Roll!

Let's Roll!
Let's Roll!
Let's keep pressing
Towards the goal.
Let's seek to spread
The light of Christ
And to destroy
The power of night.
Let's forsake wrong
And do right.
Walk in truth
And in Light.
Faithfully,
Fight the fight for Christ—
Let's Roll!

Do I Really Care?

So many faces of people I see.
I see in them longing, pain, and great need.
I have a gift for them
That God wants me to share.
The message of His love—
But do I really care?

Will I go follow Christ
Wherever He leads me?
Will I give up my life
To meet their deepest needs?

Will I let the true light
Of Jesus shine through me?
Give sacrificially
That captives may go free?

So many faces of people I see.
I see in them longing, pain, and great need.
I have a gift for them
That through God I will share.
The message of His love—
I'll give because I care.

What are Missionaries?

Based on 1 Corinthians 4:9-13, Galatians 6:9, 1 Corinthians 1:26-31 Matthew 28:18-20

Ones who are willing to be the last,
Ones who are destined to die,
Ones who are willing to be reviled,
Who by the world are despised.

Ones who are willing to be thought fools,
Spectacles made unto men,
Ones who are made the scum of the earth,
No place to dwell that's certain.

Ones who are willing to be defamed,
Who, being poor, are content.
Ones who for Christ's sake leave all behind,
Going wherever they're sent.

Ones who are willing to labor long,
Working as unto the Lord.
Ones who know how to hunger and thirst,
Bringing Good News to the world.

Ones who are willing to suffer all,
That poor, lost souls might be saved.
Ones who are emptied of all they are,
So Christ receives all the praise.

Ones who are quick to acknowledge weakness,
Waiting each day on the Lord.
Ones who continue in doing well
Confident of their reward.

These are the ones through whom God will work
To spread the Good News of Christ.
God's call is for *all* Christians to go
Filling the darkness with light.

Who will be one of these?

A Call to Go

In a poor, war-torn country,
Scarred by hatred and strife,
God calls for missionaries
To bring His love and life.

To shine the light of His Word
Into their cruel, dark night.
Sharper than a two-edged sword,
It turns hearts to the right.

Millions of unreached people
Are lost without the Lord.
Their lives are full of evil.
God's Word they have not heard.

Who will bring them the gospel
To free them from their sin?
Who will be Christ's disciple,
Seeking the lost to win?

Who will embrace the outcasts,
Seeing them through Christ's eyes,
Giving them a love that lasts,
Answering their heart cries?

I'll be that missionary!
By God's grace, I will go.
I will bless my Enemy,
Christ's love and power to show.

The road will not be easy,
It's marked by suffering,
But Jesus will stay with me,
Making my heart to sing.

One day I'll reach a country
Where tears are ever past,
Filled with God's shining glory,
Safe and secure at last.

I'll greet many people there
Whom God used me to win.
When His Good News I shared,
He drew their hearts to Him.

Together we will praise Him,
And magnify His name,
Beginning and the End,
From age to age the same!

Devotion

All of Me

Like a soldier here I stand,
Pledging all to serve my Lamb.
This Lamb was my sacrifice.
His perfect love demands my life—
My all for Jesus Christ.

Refrain:
*All of me, I give all of me
To Thee, precious Lord, to Thee.
I want others to see
Only Jesus in me,
So I'm giving all of me.*

All my plans and all my dreams,
All my heart's deepest longings,
Everything that I hold dear
I give to Thee, just draw me near.

All my talents, all my time,
All my heart and soul and mind,
Everything this world esteems,
I give it all to dwell with Thee.

All my burdens, all my fears,
All my joys and all my tears,
Every weakness that is mine
I give to Thee, my One True Vine.

My Heart is Yours

Based on Colossians 3:1, Isaiah 54:5, 1 John 5:21

My heart is Yours, Lord.
My heart is Yours.
My Maker, Husband
My heart is Yours.

Keep my eye single,
Focused on You.
Help me to please You
In all I do.

Free my affections,
Nail to Your cross.
Help me follow You
At any cost.

Teach me to trust You
In all my ways.
May my voice ever
Proclaim Your praise.

Keep me from idols
That steal my heart
Away from You. Lord,
Set me apart.

Lord, when I wander
Away from You,
Please draw me back home,
And gently woo.

Though I am weak Lord,
One thing I know.
You are my true life.
I love you so!

Surrender

We talk about surrender
But do we know what it means?
Are we willing to suffer
And give up our lives of ease?

Turning our backs on this world
To follow hard after God,
Living each day by His Word,
Led by His staff and rod,

To have no will of our own,
No secret or wrong desires,
To have eyes for Christ alone,
Buying gold, that's tried with fire,

To daily walk in His light,
Rejecting all the world's ways,
Boldly approaching the night,
Flooding it with Heaven's rays.

To say goodbye to loved ones,
And to all our hopes and dreams,
Offering our best to God's Son,
Do we know what this means?

Behold, Christ cometh soon,
Bringing His rewards with Him.
It could be at morn or at noon.
Will He find us watching then?

Or will He find a weak Church,
Consumed with earthly affairs,
A complacent, lukewarm Church,
Lifestyles that say, "I don't care."

It's easy to talk the talk,
But living it takes God's grace.
With His hand in ours we walk,
Learning to trust Him each day.

Surrender is not easy
But it is the only way.
To be happy in Jesus,
We must trust and obey.

The Runner

He runs without worry,
He runs without fear,
He runs with the knowledge
That God is near.

He strives to please Him
In all that he does,
He will not abandon
The God that he loves.

Refrain:
He is a child of the King,
His praises he'll sing,
He will an offering to Christ bring,
Of all he is, of all he has, of all he does.

My Heart's One Desire
Based on Psalm 27

To dwell all my days in the presence of my Lord,
To fix my full gaze on the beauty of my Lord,
To learn of His ways by inquiring in His Word,

This is my heart's one desire.

To seek His face,
To know Him,
Receive His grace,
To know Him,

To fear His Name,
To know Him,
To spread His fame,
To know Him,

This is my heart's one desire.

To sing His praise,
To know Him,
Feel His embrace,
To know Him,

To suffer pain,
To know Him,
Lift up His Name,
To know Him,

This is my heart's one desire.

To dwell all my days in the presence of my Lord,
To fix my full gaze on the beauty of my Lord,
To learn of His ways by inquiring in His Word,

This is my heart's one desire.

"Christian, Where's Your Scar?"

When I get to Heaven,
One by one I will see,
Those who made a difference,
And brought God's Word to me.

Those who gave up their lives,
Not counting it as loss,
Enduring hate and strife,
While taking up their cross.

Some were cruelly beaten,
Others burned in flames,
Still others were tortured,
Spit upon, and shamed.

When I see these people,
What will my tongue utter?
How will I express my thanks
For all that they suffered?

When these people see me
Will I have scars to show?
In battles for God's truth,
Did I true suffering know?

Or will I hang my head
And shamefully admit,
I chose a life of ease,
And forgot what they did?

Refrain:
Christian, where's your scar?
Show now the wounds you bore.
Christian where's your scar,
To offer to the Lord?

When I see my Savior
Who gave His all for me,
What will my tongue utter,
When His great scars I see?

None of my excuses
Will seem to matter then,
When I see the Lamb of God
Who was slain for my sin.

My Alabaster Box

Based on Matthew 26:7,13

A precious and beautiful treasure,
This alabaster box is my best,
The dearest thing on earth I possess.
Its price is beyond human measure.

This expensive box is wholly filled
With rich aromas of hopes and dreams,
Of cherished plans and deep heart longings.
Not one drop from my box may be spilled.

Clutching this treasure close to my heart,
My eyes catch a vision of the One
Whose unfailing love my heart has won,
And I know, with this box I must part.

On His head, I pour it out freely;
I release my heart's treasure to Him.
This Great One who saved me from all sin,
Poured out His precious blood all for me.

Not one earthly treasure can compare
To the treasure I have in my Lord.
Priceless, the truths I find in His Word.
Every day I become more aware

That His love is truly all I need.
In His presence my joy overflows.
Though I weep as His precious seed's sown,
My heart smiles, for much fruit I will reap.

This alabaster box is now His.
The ointment of my love, all the Lord's.
He will spread its fragrance to the world,
So all nations may know that He lives.

O Jesus, Cause Me to Love You!

From loving my life,
O Spirit set me free!
From loving this world,
Transform my thoughts to Thee.

From wrong ambitions,
Lord, loosen my tight grip.
From impure passions,
Remove away and rip.

From hatred and strife,
Overcome with your love.
From a love of wealth,
Keep my heart fixed above.

From a fear of man,
Strengthen my faith in you.
From lustful desires,
Replace with your good fruit.

From a love of sleep,
Teach me to watch and pray.
From loving pleasure,
Teach me your narrow way.

From worldly counsel,
Keep me from walking in.
From all foolishness,
Lord, give me your wisdom.

From doubt and darkness,
Let me look to your light.
From hopeless sadness,
Let me trust your way's right.

From all loneliness,
Satisfy with your love.
From weights that beset,
Give me strength to run.

Refrain:
O Jesus, cause me to love you!
With all my heart, soul, mind and strength.
With complete abandon to you,
Not looking unto lesser things.

O keep my weak, unstable soul,
Protected by your perfect law.
Use it to cleanse and make me whole
In your presence, fill me with awe.

God's care

God's Taking Care of Me

When I am alone,
No human help in sight,
All I feel is fear,
All I see is night.
That's when I choose to trust,
Believe His promises.
And though I can't see now,
The why? The when? or How?
My heart can rest,
For God knows best.

Refrain:
God's taking care of me,
My days are in His hands.
He's taking care of me,
Even when I don't understand.

When the storm clouds come,
And I can't see the light,
In my pain and tears,
I lean upon His might.
He meets me where I am,
Carries His little lamb.
Though I go through the fire,
The water and the mire,
He'll bring me out.
With joy I'll shout!

Refrain:
God's taking care of me,
And I can trust His plan.
He will fulfill His Word,
As I obey, I'll understand.

Always Know

Do you think God has forgotten?
Do you think He doesn't care?
Do you think He's far too busy
To listen to your prayer?

Don't lose heart, for at this moment
You're the object of His love.
Don't lose heart, for at this moment
He is watching from above.

Refrain:
Always know God cares for you,
And He knows all you're going through.
All His promises are true,
And He makes all things bright and new.

So when you think God has forgotten,
When you think He doesn't care,
When you think He's far too busy,
To listen to your prayer . . .

Always know God cares for you,
And He knows all you're going through.
All His promises are true,
And He makes all things bright and new.

Always know God cares for you.
Always know God cares.

A Double Rainbow

Heaven's rain began to pour,
Giving to Earth a drink.
As it rained down more and more
My soul began to sink.

For I longed to be revived
By Christ, the crucified.
Yet my sins and shortcomings
Seemed so overwhelming.

Though my heart within me failed,
His promises prevailed.
He sent down from above
An expression of His love.

A Double Rainbow . . .

The vibrant colors reached high,
Stretching across the sky.
Storm clouds and skies of gray
Began to be rolled away.

I remembered God's sweet care,
His promise to be there,
To live His life through me,
From all sin to set me free.

My heart within me sang
And praised His precious name.
He in me has overcome.
He in me the victory's won!

His great promises are true,
His mercies ever new.
The true water of His Word
Has my weary soul restored.

Everything

Based on Psalm 34:22, Hosea 2:16, and Romans 8:35

Everything, everything,
Everything you need.
Everything, everything,
Find everything in Me.

I am your source of life,
Your sufficiency.
I am your faithful guide,
Your own Prince of Peace.

No one that trusts in Me
Shall be called desolate.
Sometimes you may feel lonely.
Sometimes you may forget,

That I am . . .

Everything, everything,
Everything you need.
Everything, everything,
Find everything in Me.

I am your Bread of Life
And your own Ishi,
I am your Shining Light
And your Victory.

No one that trusts in Me
Shall be called desolate.
My love meets all your needs
And who shall separate?

Who shall separate
You from My love?

Always Satisfied

In oppressive summer heat, You are my
Cool spring.
In heavy falling snow, You are my
Covering.
In the blackness of the night, You are my
Morning Star.
In a dry and desert land, You're good news
From afar.
In the gray and rainy days, You are my
Bright rainbow.
In a forest full of prey, You are my
Safe burrow.
In the middle of the road, You are my
Steering wheel.
In the thickness of a war, You are my
Sword and shield.
Everything that I need, You are faithful
To provide.
In Your pastures I feed, and am always
Satisfied.
With You Lord, I am always satisfied!

Blessings from our Father

Our Father's surprises
Are always the best.
With love He arises
His children to bless.

His mercy and kindness
Flow down like fresh rain.
His ear inclines to us.
He calls us by name.

He knows what we need most
And offers His grace.
In His cross we boast,
While running life's race.

We run, and we fall down,
Yet, He lifts us up.
For His child there's no frown,
Only His great love.

When we least expect it,
He gives to us a song,
Reviving our spirit
Throughout the night long.

When God's face is hidden
He is still near by.
When we draw near to Him,
He draws even more nigh.

Our source of all good things
Abundantly gives
Blessings from His storehouse.
His love ever lives.

Lord, make me a blessing
To others in need,
Joyfully proclaiming
Your power to redeem!

In His Sight

Don't compare yourselves among yourselves.
Don't measure your worth by man's standards.
In the image of God, He made you.
In Christ's eyes you are of great value.

Refrain:
You are precious in His sight.
You are precious in His sight.
For your sake He bled and died.
He will never leave your side.
Oh how He loves you! Oh how He loves you!

Every person, whether great or small,
Whether young or old, God loves them all.
It's not because of the things they do,
Christ's precious blood gives each life value.

So stop striving to obtain man's praise
And start resting in God's love and grace.
When you feel that your life has no worth,
Choose to trust and believe in God's Word.

More than the Sparrow

Not one sparrow
Can fall without
God the Father.
He sees and knows
When weak humans
Fail and falter.

While lying flat
Upon the ground
In deep despair,
The child of God
Lifts up his eyes,
And breathes a prayer.

God hears his cry
And drawing close,
He pours out love.
To his poor child,
He gives hope, help,
Strength from above.

He understands
He can relate
To all our pain.
He bled and died,
Taking our place,
Bearing our shame.

The Son of God
Was fully man
And knew weakness.
As He carried
His heavy cross,
He fell, helpless.

"Take up your cross,
And follow me"
Jesus commands.
But when we try
To carry it
We cannot stand.

We are too weak
To bear our cross
Apart from Him.
For Christ alone
Delivers us
From all our sin.

His yoke's easy,
His burden light.
He will help us.
As we abide
In Christ, we are
Victorious.

God's children are
Much more to Him
Than the Sparrow.
Christ cares for us.
With Him, we can
Face tomorrow.

Waiting

Why Wait?

Based on Psalm 37:7b and James 1:4

Why wait?
Because the best and most beautiful things
Will come to those who do.

Why wait?
Because the wait is an important part
Of bearing precious fruit.

Why wait?
Because the difficult time of waiting
Helps grow and perfect you.

Why wait?
Because if God can wait for you to change
You should be patient, too.

As I Wait on You Lord

Based on Isaiah 40:29-31 and Philippians 4:13

I can't walk anymore,
I'm too weary.
I can't run anymore,
I keep falling down.
I can't climb any higher,
It's overwhelming.
For in my own power
I can do nothing.

Refrain:
But as I wait on you, Lord,
You'll renew my strength.
And as I wait on you, Lord,
You will show me—
That I can do all things
Through Christ who
Gives me His strength.
By His power working in me,
I'll overcome fully.

When doubt and darkness creep in,
My soul is troubled within,
I'll just keep looking to Him
For all the answers.
And as I gaze on His face,
Look through the light of His grace,
All doubt and darkness within
Will all fade away.

Praise

The Sacrifice of Praise
Based on Psalm 50:23

God inhabits the praises of His people.
We know from His Word that this is true.
God's great presence and peace will fill His people
As they praise Him even when it's hard to do.

We're commanded to give thanks in everything.
In joy or in sorrow, God wants us to sing.
For whoso offers praise glorifies His name.
Those who live aright will never be ashamed.

A sacrifice of praise, a sacrifice of praise,
I'll offer to the One who gave His life in my place.
There's nothing I can give to Him that ever will repay
The sacrifice Christ made when He washed my sins away.

A Song of Spring

A cool, gentle breeze caresses my face.
Sunshine floods warmth with its bright streaming rays.
The trees that surround me, show signs of spring.
Silence is broken as cheerful birds sing.

Their song is so hopeful, happy and free.
It lifts my spirit in praise, Lord to Thee.
Lord, you are my life, my strength and my song.
I yearn for Your presence all the day long.

You satisfy all of my heart's longings.
You restore, revive and cause me to sing.
With You by my side, I've no need to fear.
I rest in knowing that You're always near.

The cares of the future, I cast aside.
Nestled beneath your great wings, I abide.
Nothing can harm me, which You don't allow.
I'm safe in Your will; Your grace keeps me now.

I relish the sounds and sights of nature,
But how much more I cherish my Savior!
Though I see beauty in skies, flowers, trees,
His beauty surpasses, by far, all of these.

Songs in the Night

Singing comes so easy
When life is all carefree.
The world seems so friendly
Joining our melody.

But then true testing comes,
Bringing with it great pain.
Through the tears, we question,
"How can we sing again?"

Yet in life's darkest hour,
The nightingale's song
Comes sweetly bringing hope.
Its sound is pure and strong.

Throughout the course of time,
The loveliest of songs,
Which stir and move the soul,
Have come while night is on.

Christ, redeemed us from sin,
His life to enter in.
As our gaze shifts to Him
These songs spring from within.

A sacrifice of praise
Is in each song we raise.
Though sorrow fills our days,
We choose to trust His ways.

Sorrow

His Perfect Plan

A heart that's pierced through with sorrow,
A life that is turned upside down,
Beautiful dreams that are shattered,
God turns these all around
for good.

Refrain:
To all those who truly love Him,
Who are called by His name,
God brings beauty from the ashes,
And rainbows after rain.

God takes all the broken pieces
Of our hearts in His hand,
Using each piece to spread His love
And fulfill His perfect plan.

God's heart was pierced through with sorrow,
When on the cross Christ bore our sin.
As God's children, we must suffer,
If we will reign in Heaven
with Him.

Our hearts can rejoice through sorrow,
For our suffering can't be compared
With the glory to be revealed
Through fellowship we've shared
with Christ.

You Are My God
Based on Psalm 43:5

When life's sorrows seem much greater
Than I could ever bear,
When my heart is almost breaking,
My soul is in despair,
When I'm weak and weary
And cannot stop my tears,
I simply run to Him.

And He says . . .
Come to Me, child, come to Me.
Place your heavy burdens down at my feet.
I will never leave you, I am in control.
Be still and *know* that I am God.

I am Jehovah-Jireh—The God who provides.
No need that you have is hid from my eyes.
I am Jehovah-Rophe—The God who heals.
Although it seems impossible, my great power is real.

I am Jehovah-Shammah—The Ever Present One.
Through trials and deep suffering I won't leave you alone.
I am Jehovah-Nissi—The God of Victory.
The battles that you face each day can be won through me.

I am Jehovah-M'Kaddesh—The God of Holiness.
My child, I've set you apart, to be pure and spotless.
I am Jehovah-Shalom—The God of Perfect Peace.
When the storms of life are great, simply rest in me.

O Lord, I am coming, I'll place my hope in You.
I know You are faithful, Your promises are true.
My lips will ever praise Your holy name.
You are my God, from age to age the same.

Words of Comfort

In the stillness of night,
When all the world's asleep,
Memories fill your mind,
That sometimes makes you weep.

With every falling tear,
Remember I am here.
With every ache you feel,
Remember I can heal.

My child, I feel your pain;
I fully understand.
Through loneliness and rain
I'll always hold your hand.

Weeping may last a night
But joy comes in the morn.
When a grain of wheat dies,
New life can be born.

So hold onto My hand;
I'll help you to get through.
Someday you'll understand
My perfect plan for you.

To Laugh Again

Based on Luke 6:21b

Numbness, emptiness, sadness,
Only gray clouds in the sky.
I know God has a purpose,
But all I can ask is, "Why?"

Is life really worth living?
Will my grief ever subside?
Will I ever laugh again?
Right now, I just want to hide.

Does anyone understand
The agony of my soul,
The mute cries from my poor heart,
My longing to be made whole?

God understands the language
Of my tears and deep sorrow.
While He walked upon this earth,
Great suffering He did know.

When I have nothing to give,
That's when God can best use me
To comfort others in need,
The same way He comforts me.

By seeking to serve others,
Christ's own joy will fill my heart.
He'll surprise me with laughter
Through my tears, a smile will start.

Self-pity begins to fade
As I pray for those in need.
My night is turned into day
As God's promises I heed.

Every tear that I have shed
In His book God keeps account.
He will replace every tear
With laughter in great amounts.

Help Your Hurting People Lord!

Help your hurting people, Lord,
All across the world.
Help them know you care for them.
Help them know your Word.

Help them hear your still, small voice
Offering them hope.
Help your hurting people, Lord,
In their deep sorrow.

Help them place their trust in You
When they feel afraid.
Help them in the fight for truth
To be strong and brave.

Help them look through eyes of faith
When life seems so bleak.
Help them to rejoice in You
When their hearts grow weak.

Help your hurting people, Lord.
Help them all today.
Help your hurting people, Lord.
Hear them as they pray.

Jesus

When I Think of You Jesus

When I think of You Jesus,
My heart fills with wonder
That I, a poor sinner
Might call You my Savior.

When I think of You Jesus,
My heart fills with wonder
That You my Creator
Now call me Your daughter.

Refrain:
Your inexhaustible love,
Your incredible grace,
Your unmerited mercy,
Makes me burst into praise!

Your indescribable peace,
Your infallible truth,
Your infinite wisdom,
Jesus, I adore You!

Beautiful

Blessed Rose of Sharon,
Bloom in my heart forever.
From your beauty may I never
Cease to fix my gaze.

Fairest of Ten Thousand,
Take first place in my heart.
You are the Sun, Bright Morning Star,
Shining above all.

My beautiful Bridegroom,
You're altogether lovely.
Only your love satisfies me.
Nothing else will do.

My King in His glory
Transcends all with His light.
In His loveliness I delight.
Lesser things grow dim.

Refrain:
Beautiful! Beautiful!
My Beloved Savior
You're beautiful to me.
Beautiful! Beautiful!
Righteous, Gold of Ophir
You're beautiful to me.

The Sunshine
Based on Proverbs 4:18

The sunshine is brighter
Right after the rain.
Our Jesus seems sweeter
When we've gone through pain.

When we give Him our lives
We actually gain
His full, abundant life
And a brand new name.

Sometimes God's pathway
Is steep and hard to climb.
When we feel hopeless,
We hear a voice behind

Saying, "Child, come forth!
Put your fears aside.
Take hold of my sword.
In these words abide."

God's Word gives great strength
To follow where He leads,
Through darkness and valleys,
Through perilous seas.

His Word will give guidance,
Lighting up our way,
Giving great assurance
As we face each day.

Every day with Jesus
Is filled with great hope.
He never will forsake us
He's in full control.

He now is preparing
A place for His own.
Following God's pathway
Will lead us to home.

There Christ is the sunshine
That shines all the day.
All pain is forgotten.
Tears are wiped away.

We'll live on forever
In Heaven with Him
And worship our Savior
For days without end.

Who Are You Looking To?

Who are you looking to for answers?
Who are you looking to for peace?
Who are you hoping will fulfill
All of your heart's deepest longings?

Don't look to money for the answers.
Don't look to power or prestige.
Don't look to people to fulfill you.
Look to the Lord, He's all you need!

Refrain:
He's all you need,
In a world of uncertainty.
As you fall down upon your knees,
You will soon see,
That Jesus Christ is all you need.

What is Man?
Based on Psalm 8

When I consider
The works of Your hands,
Your love for sinners,
O Lord, what is man?

The Heavens are full
Of Your bright glory.
Why are You mindful
Of what concerns me?

The hosts of Heaven
Reveal Your greatness.
All of creation
Sounds forth Your praises.

Each star of the night,
You set in its place.
You named each one right,
To make known Your grace.

In Your great wisdom,
In Your great love,
You brought Salvation
To earth, from above.

O Lord, what is man
That You should love so?
You became a man
To rescue man's soul.

You want all to know
The power of Your love
That conquers great foes
With strength from above.

Much greater by far,
Are Your thoughts t'wards me,
Than all of the stars.
I can't hide from thee!

You know where I am,
You see in my heart.
My life's in Your hand,
Never to depart.

You call out to me,
Offering me food
To taste and to see
That You, Lord, are good.

In all of the earth,
There's no god like Thee,
Of such priceless worth,
And endless mercy.

May all that I am
Exalt Your sweet name.
You're the Risen Lamb,
Forever, the same!

To Whom Shall We Liken Him?

Based on Isaiah 40:18, Isaiah 62:5, Isaiah 66:13, Mathew 23:37, Deuteronomy 32:11, Ezekiel 34:12

To whom shall we liken our Lord—
Our Creator and King of Kings?
How inadequate are mere words
To describe One who's everything.

Oh how amazing to fathom,
This Holy One would love us so!
God, throughout all His creation,
Reveals Himself, that we might know.

He compares Himself to creatures
With attributes we understand,
That we might see a small picture
Of His loving heart and wise plan.

As a bridegroom rejoices
Over His pure, spotless bride,
So the Lord sings and rejoices
When we come to Him and abide.

As an eagle stirreth her nest,
So the Lord, in love, shakes us up,
That we might soar high and be blest,
Trusting His wings to bear us up.

As a mother comforts her child,
So the Lord, in tenderness comes
To wipe every tear with His smile.
He's the source we draw our strength from.

As a shepherd seeks out His sheep
So the Lord seeks out all His own.
He will ever guard, guide and keep,
'Till the day He brings His flock home.

As a hen gathers her chickens,
So the Lord draws us close to Him.
Beneath His wings we are hidden
And sheltered from every strong wind.

Why would we choose to reject Him—
This great Savior who loves us so?
He gave His life's blood for our sin,
Endured the cross, His love to show.

Words mis'rably fail to describe
The depth of this wonderful love.
Let us think of His wounded side
And set our affections above.

Closer Than a Brother
Based on Proverbs 18:24b

Closer than a brother
Is my Lord to me.
His love like none other
Satisfies my need.

Better far than silver,
Power, or praise could be,
More than friend or lover,
More than my family.

He is my Redeemer.
His child I'll always be.
My sin debt's gone forever
Because of Calvary.

I'll love Him forever
And serve Him faithfully.
Through all sorts of weather
He'll always walk with me.

Savior, Source, Sustainer,
Comfort, guide is He.
Closer than a brother
Is my Lord to me.

Love

No Greater Love
Based on 1 Corinthians 12:31-13:13

To daily die to self,
Putting others first,
To yield up all to God,
Future, family, health,

This is the way of love.

To bear and suffer long,
Praying with great faith,
To follow Christ's commands,
Forsaking all wrong,

This is the way of love.

To pursue holiness,
Fleeing youthful lusts,
To be the salt and light,
Seeking righteousness,

This is the way of love.

To give to others needs,
Serving selflessly,
To speak words that are kind,
Doing thoughtful deeds,

This is the way of love.

To rejoice in the truth,
Sharing it with all,
To have integrity,
Bearing precious fruit,

This is the way of love.

To forgive enemies,
Behaving with true grace,
To overlook insults,
Showing God's mercies,

This is the way of love.

To think about God's ways,
Abiding in Him,
To let Him lead and guide,
Trusting in His grace,

This is the way of love.

To be spent and to spend,
Laying down one's life,
To sacrifice and give,
This love has no end.

There is no greater love.

The Wonder of Your Love

Oh Lord, how quickly I forget
Just who you truly are.
I get impatient and upset
When from my thoughts You're far.

When all my focus is on me
I cannot worship You.
Thinking of all my perceived needs,
I ignore what is true.

The truth that You are holy, Lord,
You're worthy of all praise,
That You are faithful, Lord,
Full of love, truth and grace.

By keeping my mind stayed on You
I have Your perfect peace
And when I trust and obey too,
It brings such sweet release.

Refrain:
May the wonder of Your love
Never cease to amaze me!
Fix my eyes on things above.
From all idols set me free.

May my heart's deepest desire
Be to glorify Your name.
Though it means refining fire,
May I never bring You shame!

Lord, You paid the full price for me;
You suffered in my place.
Giving Your life, not just for me,
But for the human race.

Fill my heart with the greatest awe
As I remember You.
May my heart delight in Your law
And find it ever new.

When I begin to turn away,
Taking my eyes off You,
Choosing to go my own, wrong way,
Then, Savior, gently woo.

Teach me to abide in Your words,
Dying to my own self,
To let You be my only Lord,
Serving You, nothing else.

Refrain:
May the wonder of Your love
Guard, guide and safely keep me
From the pride and worldly lust
Which easily besets me.

May I shed Your love abroad
To all those who hate Your name.
As they see Your love, O God,
May they call upon Your Name.

The King's Daughter

A poor and needy girl
Dressed in filthy rags,
Walked down a lonely road,
Her eyes dark and sad.

Her whole future seemed bleak,
Filled with great despair.
She cried, "Help, Lord, I'm weak!"
Then, He met her there.

Her life began to change
When she gazed on His face.
She felt her troubles fade
As He spoke words of grace.

My dear, precious daughter,
If only you knew
How long I've sought after
And deeply loved you!

I've been waiting so long
For you to call me,
Forsaking what's wrong,
Letting me be King.

You are my own Princess—
The child of my love.
For you, I sent Jesus—
My Son, from above.

He is your Prince of Peace.
He gave His own blood
To save and set you free.
How great is His love!

You have now a new name,
No longer your own.
My grace you can claim,
As heir to my throne.

Now as the King's Daughter,
You're glorious within.
Child, always remember,
You are dead to sin!

Your garments are spotless,
They glisten like gold.
Clothed in Christ's righteousness,
Come sing and be bold!

You have nothing to fear,
I am in control.
I want you to draw near,
To be still and know.

With her heart full of hope,
The princess drew near.
Bowing before His throne,
She shed grateful tears.

Her life changed forever,
With reason to sing,
She lived ever after,
Adoring her King.

Loved by God

When I feel so utterly
Unlovable,
Wondering why Almighty God
Loves me at all . . .

Then, from His fountain filled with blood,
I drink, plunge deep beneath the flood.
My life is hid with Christ in God,
He makes me worthy of His love.

When I feel this just can't be
Then I ponder
The cruel cross of Calvary
And know for sure.

God loves me as His very own
And not for merits that I have done.
I stand clothed in Christ's righteousness,
Assured of His full acceptance.

When my feelings tell me things
That are not true,
I will cling to God's pure Word
Which makes me new.

His faithful promises to me
Give hope, despite life's uncertainty.
On Christ, the solid Rock I stand.
All else is nothing but sinking sand.

A Love That Hurts

Like a dagger that pierces deep
Into a bleeding soul,
Such great depth, causing us to weep,
Hearts can't contain the whole.

Yet from the pain of this great love
Comes sweet healing and power
Sent from our Father above,
Filling us with wonder.

Wonder, that the Almighty God
Would condescend to be
Born as a babe upon earth's sod,
Then die upon a tree.

To rescue poor, dying people,
From the bondage of sin,
Offering life and renewal,
Hope and peace within.

The Father's heart was broken
As His beloved Son cried.
Since Holiness could not view sin,
Alone, Christ bled and died.

It should come as no surprise then,
That it hurts when we love,
For sacrifice and suffering
Are what love is made of.

God's chastening has many forms,
Trials of diverse kinds.
For every child into Christ born,
They're part of His design.

Trials are meant to test our faith,
To see if we'll endure,
Stripping all of our pride away
Until our hearts are pure.

God does not afflict willingly,
Or bruise children of men.
He wants us to trust completely
And find our strength in Him.

We love Him because He loved us,
And paid sin's costly price.
If we will follow our Jesus,
It will mean sacrifice.

And now, behold a mystery:
Christ and His glorious bride,
United for eternity,
In God's love to abide.

All pain and tears are passed away
As we sing love's glad song,
For every child into Christ born,
They're part of His design.

Empty Me

Empty me, Lord, empty me!
Fill my heart only with Thee.
Strip away my foolish pride.
In your love, may I abide.

Your love is selfless and kind.
Your love is giving, all the time.
Your love is patient and true.
Your love is never proud or rude.

Your love endures under stress.
Your love withstands all trials and tests.
Your love serves the "least of these".
Your love will stoop to wash their feet.

Empty me, Lord, empty me!
Teach me your humility.
May the love of Jesus Christ
Rule in me throughout this life.

Your love is quick to forgive.
Your love shows us all how to live.
Your love is not envious.
Your love seeks every day to bless.

Your love will never condemn.
Your love is grieved over my sin.
Your love rejoices in truth.
Your love seeks to renew my youth.

Empty me, Lord, empty me!
Let my life be spent for Thee.
Filled with your love's power divine,
May your light through my life shine.

With An Everlasting Love

In every human heart
There's a longing to be loved,
A longing to be cherished
Simply for who you are.

Search the whole world over,
Yet no mortal can be found,
Whom perfect love can offer.
Christ alone is this love's fount.

To every longing soul,
God's sweet message is the same,
To come and receive His name
And know His love in full.

Refrain:
With an everlasting love
I have loved you.
With an everlasting love
I have bought you.
With an everlasting love
I have chosen you
To bear much fruit
For my glory.

Trust

Do You Trust Me?

So softly, gently, intently,
God's voice to my heart speaks.
This question, He asks me simply,
"My child, do you *trust* Me?"

Do you trust Me?
When you can't see any way out,
When the sunshine's covered with clouds,
When you're tempted to fear and doubt,
Do you trust Me?

Do you trust Me?
When it seems like no one else cares,
When your heart fails and starts to despair,
When you can't even offer a prayer,
Do you trust Me?

Do you trust Me?
When the answers just aren't enough,
When life's road is steep and rough,
When you're emptied of human love,
Do you trust Me?

Do you trust Me?
When waiting seems like agony,
When you must die to all your dreams,
When you have *nothing* left but Me,
Do you trust Me?

I've come to give you life,
Abundant life and free.
The only way to live
Is to abide in Me.

My plans for your life are the best,
To give you an abundant hope
Of eternal life and sweet rest,
Of joy and a Heavenly home.

As my heart listens to His voice
I know that I must make a choice.
I choose to trust God and His plan,
Believe His Word and take His Hand.

Through my tears I look up to Him
And feel His peace and joy within.
Though at times the future seems bleak,
In Him, I find all that I seek.

God's Unexpected Gift

When God's gift is not what I expected,
When His answer seems strange to my ear,
When His calling seems so overwhelming,
When I grapple with questions and fear,

I know this gift is what I have longed for,
The fulfillment of my heart's desire.
It is what I have waited so long for,
Yet it comes at an unlikely hour.

This gift brings to me major life changes
Shaking me out of my comfort zone,
Calling me to go to unknown places
A long distance from family and home.

What is my response to God for this gift?
Do I receive it with thankfulness,
Or do I allow my strong emotions
To consume me and bring me distress?

The great Father of Lights can be trusted,
For He never makes any mistakes.
All the gifts that He gives us are good gifts;
He will bind up each heart that He breaks.

He will grant enough grace for the journey,
His presence will go with me each day.
I need never fear when He calls my name,
I need only to trust and obey.

Trust me for Today

Lord, right now I feel so overwhelmed,
I don't know where to turn.
I don't know what to do.
I have so much to learn!

Lord, right now the future frightens me,
With all the great unknowns,
With all of life's pressures,
While all creation groans.

Lord, my restless heart cries out to you!
I hear your gentle chide:
"My child, cease your striving,
Come to me and abide."

Just trust me for today.
Just trust me for today.
Through this vast wilderness,
I will make a way.

Just trust me for today.
Just trust me for today.
I will direct your paths,
As you yield and obey.

Lord, right now my heart rejoices
As I think on your truth,
As I rest in your love,
As I magnify you.

Lord, thank you for your great promises
That never, never, fail.
The truth of your pure Word
Will ever more prevail.

I'll trust you for today.
I'll trust you for today.
Through this vast wilderness,
You will make a way.

I'll trust you for today.
I'll trust you for today.
You will direct my paths,
As I yield and obey.

Changes

Changes, changes,
Every day.
Things of this earth
Quickly pass away.
But Jesus is faithful.
He remains the same.
He never changes—Praise His Holy Name!
He never changes—Praise His Holy Name!

In life's seasons,
There's joy and pain.
Sometimes there's sunshine,
Sometimes there is rain.
People we love will
Come and go, yet
Jesus stays with us—He'll never let go!
Jesus stays with us—He'll never let go!

Trust Him, trust Him,
Every day.
There's a purpose
In every change He makes.
He who began the
Good work in you,
He will perform it—I know that it's true!
He will perform it—I know that it's true!

His Way

So many choices,
So many roads,
So many voices,
So many loads.

Oh where do I go?
What should I do?
Oh how can I know
The way that is true?

The answers I need
Are found in Christ.
As His Word I read,
My path has light.

When I can't see
The steps ahead,
My Shepherd guides me.
By His hand I'm led.

Through Baca's valley,
Through waters deep,
Through difficulty,
He'll guard and keep.

Keep me from evil,
Keep me from harm,
Keep me in His will,
Free from alarm.

He will perfect all
That concerns me.
He hears when I call.
He gives me peace.

So I'll face today,
Sustained by grace.
God has made a way
To run this race.

I'll acknowledge Him
With trusting heart.
His way I'll walk in
And not depart.

For Good

What good, thought some, could ever come
From Slavery?
They could not see, in misery,
God's plan to make a strong nation.

What good, thought some, could ever come
From Nazareth?
They could not see, could not believe,
The Messiah had truly come.

What good, thought some, could ever come
From an old cross?
They could not see, could not conceive
Christ's death would bring our salvation.

What good, thought some, could ever come
From violent storms?
They could not see, Christ on the Sea,
To teach them a faith-filled lesson.

Whatever comes, let's trust God's Son,
For He's with us.
Though we can't see God's tapestry,
We know that He is sovereign.

Refrain:
And we know that all things, all things,
Work together for good
To them that love God,
To them who are called
According to His purpose.
(Repeat)

Eyes of Faith

Each one of us must choose what he'll believe,
In things our eyes can see or what's unseen,
Things we understand or cannot fathom,
In the Word of God or human reason.

The choice is up to us, whom will we trust?
Will we look to ourselves or to Jesus?
God made the Universe; He's over all.
He knew us before birth; On Him we call.

When we call on His name in child-like faith,
We'll never be the same for His blood saves.
Though fear may come at times; we see great waves,
Christ will ease our minds, if we have faith.

Refrain:
With eyes of faith we will see light
While those around us grope in night.
With eyes of faith we will have hope
That Christ will conquer every foe.

He controls all the waves; in Him we trust,
Believe His words by faith and do what's just.
The One who has the power over the seas,
Is the One who fully should control me.

This life on earth is not all that there is.
The greatest part is still yet to be.
And our rewards in heaven will be rich,
If we now will seek Him diligently.

Treasures of the Darkness

When the darkness closes in,
Casting shadows 'cross my way,
When my vision grows all dim,
So I cannot see the day,

When my failures and my sins
Are revealed in deeper ways,
When I want to hide from Him,
Then I hear my Father say:

My child, draw near,
Don't close your heart.
Bow down your ear,
I won't depart.

I am with you,
I'll heal, restore,
Make your heart new,
Forevermore.

The treasures of the darkness
Are revealed when I believe
In God's precious promises
And with child-like faith receive.

There is no form of darkness
That His light can't overcome.
He is a mighty fortress,
A strong shelter from the storm.

The secret place of thunder
Is where He'll answer me.
When I choose to surrender,
Then His power I'll receive.

Though I pass through the valley
Of the shadow of death,
His full life will revive me.
In His love is perfect rest.

I will not fear the darkness,
But trust in the light of God.
He can see through the darkness;
He brings comfort with his rod.

Looking back on this journey,
I'll recall God's Sovereign hand.
Hidden riches will I see,
And His heart I'll understand.

Let Me See Jesus

Lord, give me eyes
To see Your face
In every person
That comes my way.

Give me Your eyes
To see their needs
And how to meet them,
Forgetting me.

Lord, give me ears
To hear Your voice,
Then obey promptly
With inner joy.

Give me Your ears
To hear the cry
Of every hurting
And hopeless life.

Lord, give me faith
To come to You,
To walk on water,
And find You true.

Give me Your faith
When I can't see
Just how You're working
Out Your plan in me.

Lord, let me see
Eternity.
Lord, let me hear
Your voice so near.

Lord, let me trust
That You're enough.
Let me see Jesus.

Lift Up Your Eyes

Are you weighed down
By worry and fear,
Wondering how
Jesus could be near?

Does your problem
Seem overwhelming?
Feeling too broken
To praise God, and sing?

Lift up your eyes
From whence comes your help.
Come and arise.
Turn your gaze from self.

Look unto Christ.
He will give you rest.
Let go of sin
And reach for His best.

His promises
Will never fail you.
The Word He gives
Is faithful and true.

Don't ever doubt
The depth of His love.
Pour your heart out
Before God above.

Looking to Him,
Life's problems seem small.
This world grows dim
As He becomes all.

Great and Precious Promises

Great and precious promises
Of them God's Word is full.
Each one of them is certain.
To doubt, I'd be a fool.

When my heart grows discouraged
And all I see is night,
Then I go back to God's Word.
He points me to the light.

The promise of His presence
Is music to my ears.
Whenever I feel lonely,
I trust that He is near.

When my sins and shortcomings
Fill my heart with sadness,
Then I confess and cling to
His promise of forgiveness.

When I feel worn and weary,
Too tired to go on,
Then His promise of rest
Brings to my heart a song.

When this world oppresses me,
I long for Heav'n and home.
The promise of His coming
Is what I stand upon.

For every season of life,
There's a promise to claim,
Making each day a delight
As I trust in His name.

What God has said, He will do.
Jesus will never fail.
His mercies each day are new.
His promises prevail!

The Impossible is Possible

An old married couple
Were far past child-bearing years.
When told they would bear a son,
They scarce believed their ears.

Abraham and Sarah
Had lives full of surprises.
One thing they knew for certain,
God keeps his promises.

Ninety one years of age,
Sarah gave birth to her son.
Isaac, the child of promise,
Became a great nation.

The impossible is possible
When we choose to trust in God.
The impossible is possible
When we choose to trust in God.

A small, young shepherd boy
Knew something had to be done.
The great giant Goliath
Was boasting he had won.

The army of Israel
Hid, paralyzed by fear.
They would not face the giant,
But David volunteered.

His hope was in the Lord.
With confidence God would win,
Young David faced Goliath,
And with a stone, slew him.

The impossible is possible
When we choose to trust in God.
The impossible is possible
When we choose to trust in God.

An orphaned, Jewish girl,
Married to a heathen King;
Appealing for her people,
Could be life threatening.

Yet Esther trusted God.
Stepping bravely out in faith,
She went before the king,
Leaving to God her fate.

The king's heart turned t'ward her
And he granted her request.
In time, the Jewish people
Could live in peace and rest.

The impossible is possible
When we choose to trust in God.
The impossible is possible
When we choose to trust in God.

A blind man sat begging,
As the multitude passed by.
When he heard Jesus coming,
Loudly he did cry.

Others tried to stop him.
He cried louder for mercy.
Then standing near, Christ asked him,
"What shall I do for thee?"

"My sight", pled the beggar.
He received far more than this.
Through faith in Christ he was saved.
What gleeful joy was his!

The impossible is possible
When we choose to trust in God.
The impossible is possible
When we choose to trust in God.

Two Christian apostles
Were cruelly beaten.
With their feet bound fast in stocks,
They were cast in prison.

Paul and Silas praised God,
Singing throughout that dark night.
God sent a major earthquake.
No more were they bound tight.

The jailer was afraid,
But Paul set his mind at ease.
The jailer and his family
Then on the Lord believed.

The impossible is possible
When we choose to trust in God.
The impossible is possible
When we choose to trust in God.

For all of God's children
There will be trials and tests.
If we only see the bad,
Then we will miss God's best.

God wants us to see life
Through the eyes of child-like faith,
Looking past all our problems
Into His wondrous face.

As we look upon Him
Doubt and darkness disappear.
There is no hopeless sadness
When our Lord is so near.

The impossible is possible
When we choose to trust in God.
The impossible is possible
When we choose to trust in God.

Repentance

Grace to the Humble
Based on James 4:6 and 2 Chronicles 7:14

In our crazy, confused world,
For true help, where does one turn?
All around us darts are hurled!
Truth is looked upon with scorn.

Tolerance, conformity
Are society's virtues.
Everything focused on *me*,
With eyes blind to real issues.

Embracing all religions
But rejecting Jesus Christ.
Listening to man's opinions,
Excusing all the vice.

Our nation has forgotten
The true God who made her great.
We no longer blush at sin.
His holy standards we hate.

If we don't return to God,
He will bring swift destruction.
One stroke of His chast'ning rod
Will show us He is sov'reign.

But if, in humility,
We will pray and seek God's face,
Confess our iniquity,
And turn from our wicked ways,

Then will He hear from Heaven,
Grant forgiveness for our sin.
As we place our trust in Him,
Our land's healing can begin.

Refrain:
God resisteth the proud
But giveth grace unto the humble.
God resisteth the proud
But giveth grace to the humble.

Song of America

Many years ago
They left their home
In England, to come
To a new land called
America—
A place of freedom,

Where they could worship
The one, true God,
No fear of arrest.
They stepped out in faith,
Looking to God,
Enduring each test.

In America
They now were free
From England's cruel King.
Giving thanks to God
For all He'd done,
They began to sing.

America, America
You're the land that I love.
Your greatness came from the right hand
Of the great God above.

Now as God's children,
We are pilgrims.
We're seeking a home
Where our trials will end,
Free from all sin,
Never more to roam.

Let us seek to win
Lost souls for Him,
Leading them to Christ
Let us lay aside
Each weight and claim
The glorious prize.

To a Higher Power,
We give honor.
Jesus is King.
When He's in control
Of heart and soul,
Then we're free to sing.

America, America
You're the land that I love.
Your greatness came from the right hand
Of the great God above.

When you sought His face,
He poured His grace
Down from Heav'n above.
You were separate.
God made you great,
A witness of His love.

But now you have lost sight of Him
To whom your life you owe.
You've forgotten the faithful men
Who died, that you might know

The beauty of self government,
One nation under God,
With freedom, peace, and brotherhood,
With Liberty for all.

America, America,
Turn your heart back to God,
Or else, He will bring swift judgment
With His chastening rod.

America, America,
You're much too young to die!
Repent now, and turn back to God
And He will hear your cry.

The Shepherd and His Lamb

Like a little lost lamb I've wandered
Far away from my Shepherd's embrace.
Such precious time has been squandered
As I've turned away from His dear face.

Delighting in temporal pleasures
Which fail to fully satisfy.
Believing that my earthly treasures
Will answer my heart's desperate cry.

Yet as my Good Shepherd, He woos me,
Safely leading me back to His fold,
Seeing past all my stupidity,
To a lamb who is hungry and cold.

He offers me complete forgiveness
When I humbly repent of my sin.
His strength is made perfect in weakness.
He helps me to start over again.

What a wonderful and good Shepherd,
To so tenderly care for His own.
His great love fills me with gratitude.
Glory to God for all He has done!

The Light of Jesus

Disaster, disease, deception, despair,
The horrors of death appear everywhere.
Yet in such great darkness, a light appears.
It's presence brings peace that drives away fear.

Refrain:
The light of Jesus
Shines in the night.
Calling all sinners,
Turn to the right.

Repent of your sins.
Look to the cross.
Confess Christ as Lord.
Count all things as loss.

The world around us grows darker each day.
Those who reject Christ have Hell's price to pay.
As sons of God, we must proclaim His Word
To untold millions who have never heard.

Peace

Be Still and Know
Based on Psalm 46:10

See the chaos that surrounds us.
Hear the noisome pestilence,
Voices seeking to confound us
With their threatening presence.

Though we are faced with war and strife,
We need never be afraid,
For we know the Giver of Life.
In our trouble, He's our aid.

In a world of catastrophes,
We have this blessed, sure hope.
The God to whom we bow our knees
Is high upon His throne.

His words speak comfort to our souls,
His presence quiets our hearts.
Though sorrows like sea billows roll,
His sweet peace never departs.

If we will take the time to listen,
Come aside and rest awhile,
We will hear Christ's invitation
To make Him our all in all.

***Refrain:**
Be still and know that I am God. (x2)
I will be exalted among the heathen;
I will be exalted in the earth. (x2)*

Be of Good Cheer

Based on John 16:33

Tears fill my eyes
When I see all the vice
In the world around me.

My heart grows faint
When I see all the pain
In world around me.

Every day brings
All sorts of suffering
Which can overwhelm me.

Refrain:
In the world ye shall have tribulation,
In the world ye shall have tribulation,
But be of good cheer!
Be of good cheer!
I have overcome the world.

One thing I know,
We will reap what we sow,
From good or from bad seeds.

Those who love Christ
Will reap eternal life
And know true joy and peace.

I need not fear
When my Lord is so near
He will never leave me.

His Word is true.
All He says He will do.
He is greater in me,

Greater than sin,
Greater than him
Who is my Enemy.

Disappointments

Life is full of disappointments,
Of broken plans and dreams,
But these are just God's instruments
To help make our hearts clean.

When everything is stripped away,
Then finally we can see
That Jesus is the only Way
To life and joy and peace.

When we are satisfied in Him
Our troubles seem so small.
We find that He is our best friend
When we surrender all.

Endurance

Get Up!

Are you fallen?
Then get up!
Don't lie there on the ground.

Are you broken?
Then look up!
With Christ, healing is found.

Are you barren?
Don't give up!
In Christ, fruit will abound.

Refrain:
Get up, look up, don't you give up!
There is a fight to win!
Our foes are great, our God they hate,
But our strength is in Him!

Are you thirsty?
Fill your cup!
Drink from Christ's blood-filled fount.

Are you hungry?
Come and sup!
In His Word, food is found.

Are you lonely?
Then cheer up!
Christ's presence does surround.

Refrain:
Fill cup, cheer up, come and sup up!
It's time to face the day.
O'er mountains steep, through valleys deep
Our God will make a way!

Before Sunset

The hours just before sunset
Are brief and bittersweet.
The fight is not yet over
Though victory's guaranteed.

On, on the battle rages.
We dare not call retreat.
In these hours before sunset
We must be strong, not weak.

As good soldiers of Jesus
Let's serve Him faithfully.
Fight with a single purpose,
Live for eternity.

Knowing beyond the sunset
A great, bright city gleams,
Where Jesus reigns forever,
What glory that will be!

When we are with our Savior
We'll worship at His feet,
Our troubles gone forever,
Our joy in Him complete.

Until then, let's keep fighting
With all our might to win,
These short hours before sunset,
The crown of life from Him.

Your Grace

Lord,
I can't love unselfishly,
I can't give all cheerfully,
I can't trust you completely,
Apart from your grace.

My springs would run all dry.
I'd fall each time I tried.
I'd give up with a sigh,
Apart from your grace.

Refrain:
Your grace is sufficient for me.
Your grace gives me victory.
Your strength is made perfect in my weakness.
So most gladly will I glory
In each trial and infirmity,
That your power may rest upon me.
Your grace is sufficient for me.

Lord,
When the pressure is so strong,
To leave you and do what's wrong,
I know that where sin abounds,
Grace much more abounds.

I can live with great hope,
You'll never let me go,
You will keep your own,
By your truth and grace.

Hold On!

As a disciple of Christ,
The conflict will be keen.
With great forces we must fight,
With darkness that's unseen.

When for Christ we take our stand,
With His love as our theme,
The world will not understand.
To them, foolish we seem.

Each day we face many cares,
And our numbers seem small.
We are tempted to despair
And to let our arms fall.

The Enemy of our souls
Wants to see us retreat,
To doubt God is in control,
To know fear and defeat.

We must not turn back from Christ
Though the battle goes long.
We must not flee from the fight.
To Him, we must hold on!

Refrain:
Hold on! Hold on!
Victory is nigh.
Though the wait seems long,
Look up to the sky!
He'll come! He'll come!
To receive His bride.
He will take her home
Ever to abide.

When our feet begin to slip,
His arms will carry us.
When our fingers lose their grip,
His pierced hand will grasp us.

Christ will never let us go.
In Him we are secure.
He will conquer every foe.
His promises are sure.

Until our Bridegroom cometh
Let's serve Him faithfully.
We need have no fear of death,
We'll live eternally!

Let Us Not Be Weary
Based on Galatians 6:9

The daily cares of life
Seek to pull us down.
The world with all it's strife
Can turn life upside down.

When no one understands,
It seems we're all alone,
When fallen are our hands,
And we long to be home.

We must remember this,
That God is on His throne.
The victory is His.
We're not left on our own!

Refrain:
Let us not be weary
In well doing.
Let us not be weary
In well doing.
For in due season we shall reap,
If we faint not.
For in due season we shall reap,
If we faint not!

God's grace will meet our need,
Give strength to face each day.
His Holy Word we read
To guide us all the way.

Encouragement we find
By trusting in His Word,
Leaving our doubts behind,
And clinging to our Lord.

Let us pass on this hope,
Encouraging each other.
Through prayer, holding the ropes,
Singing though we suffer.

Lest any one of us
Become hardened by sin,
Let us look to Jesus,
Abide always in Him.

Let us live faithful lives
In this ungodly world.
Keep reaching for the prize
Which is in Christ our Lord!

Run On!

The finish line is just in sight.
The race is almost done.
We ask the Lord to give us might
To fix our gaze and run.

Though fallen men are all around,
We will not turn aside.
For the Promised Land we are bound,
In Christ's love we abide.

The taunts and jeers of this old world
Have no power over us.
Though Satan's darts at us are hurled,
Our strong shield is Jesus.

It won't be long before we're home,
All troubles will be o'er.
Though we've still miles yet to roam,
Christ awaits at the door.

Let us endure until the end,
So no one takes our crown.
Let us all live to honor Him
And at His feet bow down.

Refrain:
Run on!
Run on!
Run on for Christ!
Keep reaching for the prize.
Be strong!
Be strong!
Be strong in Christ!
Let no one take your prize.

The Mountain Climb

After living in the valley with its comforts and its cares,
Dwelling in the lower lands with their small ambitions,
My soul becomes dissatisfied with where I've settled,
And deeply desires the abundant life which Christ freely shares.

From a distance I see mountain tops which seem to touch the sky.
A longing to reach those heights wells up inside my heart.
Sprinting toward a mountain, I begin the great ascent,
Quickly discovering it is not easy to climb up high.

Every step is difficult, requiring concentration.
My progress is slow and my heart burns hot within me.
No matter how hard I try, my feet keep on slipping.
The process is painful and fills me with frustration.

In my despair I ignore all the beauty that surrounds me.
Across the rocky mountainside, wildflowers are strewn.
Their presence teaches lessons of thriving in hardship.
If I will choose to accept it, there is joy for the journey.

If I had wings I could fly up high and swiftly reach the top,
  But I would miss the blessings that come along the way.
 The sweetest blessings only come through tears, toil and pain.
  With one step at a time, I press on, determined not to stop.

 Though I cannot always see Him, my Shepherd guides me,
   Ordering all of my steps according to His will.
  With delight He perfects my weakness into His strength.
One day the mountain mist will lift and His smiling face I'll see.

 It is the process, not the outcome, that God cares most about.
    Daily He's conforming me into His own image.
   Like a parent who takes pride in his baby's first steps,
   Over all His dear children, the Lord does sing and shout.

My Lord does not see me as I am, weak, crippled, and confused.
    He sees me as I am in Him, complete and perfect.
   He who began the good work in me will complete it.
   Upon this precious promise I often meditate and muse.

God's Way

Sometimes I want to run away,
Don't want to face another day.
Still I will choose to go God's way
And learn to walk by faith.

Sometimes the end is not in sight
And I am overcome with fright.
Engulfed by shadows of the night,
I trust the God of Light.

In Him, there is no need to fear.
His presence is forever near.
He gently wipes away each tear.
His love, my heart does cheer.

Refrain:
God's Way
God's Way
God's Way is higher than my way!
He knows
He knows
He knows every path that I take.

My Savior did not run away.
He endured each step of the way.
And joyfully, He did obey,
Dying, my debt to pay.

To earth He came to seek and save
And now He's risen from the grave!
His voice can calm each crashing wave.
In His love, I am safe.

Prayer

Praying People

Like arrows that are shot
With precision to Heav'n,
Reaching the heart of God,
Putting faith in action,

Are the deep fervent prayers
Offered by God's children,
With sacrifice and tears,
Vials of odors, golden.

This secret discipline
Is often neglected.
It's hard to fit it in,
We often rush ahead,

Trying to solve problems
In our own human strength,
Not acknowledging Him,
Not taking time to seek.

More than anything else,
Prayer changes us.
As we cry out for help,
Christ pours His grace on us.

When we stop to listen
To His still and small voice,
Our hearts are turned to Heav'n,
We can't help but rejoice.

Praying causes God's plan,
To unfold before our eyes.
Though we don't understand,
We know it's good and wise.

Whatever we may ask,
In faith, we'll receive.
God will show us great things
If we will but believe.

Sometimes we may wonder,
"Did God hear what we prayed?"
God does not slumber.
We need not be dismayed.

The answers God gives us
May be hard to accept.
In His love, we must trust,
For He knows what is best.

All around us we see
People burdened with care.
Praying ones we must be,
Waging a great warfare,

Against powers of darkness,
Claiming Christ's victory,
Praying with humbleness,
Praying unceasingly,

Yielding fully to Him,
And to His perfect will,
Renouncing our sin,
Letting His Spirit fill.

As God's praying people,
We'll transform history,
Through faith that is simple,
We will "part the Red Sea".

A Missionary's Prayer

Lord, break my heart
With all the things that break Your heart.
Lord, give me Your
Eyes of compassion for the world.

Lord, I release
Desires for happiness and ease.
Lord, Your true way
Will include suffering and pain.

Lord, give me grace
To daily fall upon my face.
Lord, keep me from
All weights which make it hard to run.

Lord, I find in You
The power for everything I do.
Lord, You alone
Are my strong Rock and Cornerstone.

Lord, I am Yours.
In Your great love I am secure.
Lord, may I be
Your shining light to those I see.

Lord, may they come,
Placing their trust in You alone.
Lord, guard and keep
The precious souls who are Your sheep.

Lord, keep me safe
Until I reach my resting place.
Lord, may I sing
Of Your great power to redeem.

The One Thing Needful

So many projects to be done,
So many needs to meet,
People screaming for attention,
These things can smother me.

That is when I must remember,
The one thing that I need.
It's to draw close to my Savior
Listening at His feet.

His words bring me hope and comfort
Reminding me again,
The one thing that's most important,
Is fellowship with Him.

Laundry, dishes, papers to grade,
Visitors, piles to do,
I roll my burdens on to Him,
And He will pull me through.

If I major on the minor,
Then I'll miss my Savior's voice.
Focusing on what's temporal
Is making a poor choice.

I choose to lay aside my cares,
My burdens, doubts and fears,
Taking them to my Lord in prayer,
Confidant He will hear.

Prayer puts life in God's perspective,
Bringing rest to my soul.
As I come near and learn of Him,
He makes everything whole.

Call Upon Me
Based on Psalm 50:15

When your heart is lonely
And your fears are strong,
When your needs are pressing
And you can't go on,
That's when I am waiting
To hear your humble cry.
I am your Good Shepherd,
And I'm always nigh.

When you feel so helpless
And the pressure's on,
When it seems impossible
And your strength's all gone,
That's when I can show you
I am all in all.
My strength is made perfect
In you as you call.

Refrain:
*And call upon me (x3)
In the day of trouble
I will deliver thee (x3)
And thou shalt glorify Me.*

When the future frightens you
And the valley's low,
When your friends all leave you
You feel all alone,
I will stick beside you
Through the darkest night,
Leading you and guiding you
To my perfect light.

Oh my child I love you.
You belong to Me.
I've redeemed you with my blood
And I've set you free.
I will show you mighty things
Which you cannot know.
If you call upon Me
I will make it so.

When you've given everything
To serve Me faithfully,
When you've let me use you
To meet countless needs,
Then someday—in Heaven,
At my throne you'll fall.
There you will see clearly
It was worth it all.

Edwards Brothers,Inc!
Thorofare, NJ 08086
24 November, 2010
BA2010329